Original title:
Sapling Scribbles

Copyright © 2025 Creative Arts Management OÜ
All rights reserved.

Author: Nora Sinclair
ISBN HARDBACK: 978-1-80567-335-4
ISBN PAPERBACK: 978-1-80567-634-8

Green Pen and Paper

In a garden of thoughts, I doodle a tree,
With leaves made of laughter, oh so carefree.
A squirrel in a bowtie, quite dapper indeed,
Chasing down acorns for his stylish speed.

My pen starts to giggle, the ink takes a leap,
Drawing clouds that whisper, secrets they keep.
A sun in sunglasses, shining so bright,
Waving to flowers that dance in pure delight.

Sketching Shadows of Tomorrow

With crayons of sunshine, I outline my dreams,
A rabbit with sneakers, or so it seems.
The trees wear their glasses, all wise and astute,
While grasshoppers sketch in their snazzy little suits.

The horizon winks back, with a cheeky little grin,
As I paint a new world where whimsy begins.
Turtles on rollerblades wobble with glee,
Chasing after rainbows, that's just how it be.

Fragments of Flora's Story

In the pages of petals, I write with a quill,
A bee in a top hat insists on the thrill.
With whispers of wind, I capture the sound,
Of giggles from blossoms that twirl all around.

Each stem tells a tale, both funny and bright,
Of daisies that dance under soft moonlight.
A stubborn old fern, with a witty remark,
Marks where the fairies plan their fun in the dark.

Chronicles Beneath the Canopy

Beneath leafy layers, the stories unfold,
Of critters in costumes, both daring and bold.
A raccoon with a crown, king of his scene,
Directs all the squirrels in a show, oh so keen!

With each rustle of leaves, a chuckle arrives,
As fireflies twinkle, like stars in disguise.
The grass hums a tune, sweet as can be,
Where laughter and magic dance joyfully free.

New Leaves of Reflection

When leaves first burst, they dance so bright,
Each wiggle and twist, a comical sight.
They squabble with bugs, play tag with the breeze,
Oh, to be young with such silly degrees.

A tree with a hat made of sunlight and dew,
Chasing the clouds, what a silly view!
It chuckles as branches tickle the sky,
While squirrels crack jokes, as they scamper by.

With each little bud, there's laughter anew,
Spreading like gossip, there's plenty to view.
They jest about rain and the mud that it brings,
In the grand game of nature, oh how the chorus sings!

Fresh green comedy, a sight to behold,
Tiny, bold stories from the young and the old.
They flip and they flop, in the summer's warm light,
These leaves full of giggles, oh what pure delight!

Whispers in the Wind

The wind tells secrets, a mischievous muse,
Whirling and twirling, with nothing to lose.
It tickles the flowers, a giggle or two,
And plays hide and seek with the skies, how it flew!

A leafy debate on who's the most green,
With a chorus of rustles, the gossip is keen.
They joke 'bout the rain, and how they all pout,
For a splash in the puddles, that's what it's about!

Branches all chuckle, as they sway in a row,
Imitating dancers with laughter to show.
A twirl and a spin, oh what fun it may be,
To revel together in nature's grand spree!

So come join the laughter, where trees intertwine,
The whispers of breezes, a ticklish design.
In the heart of the forest, where joy does reside,
Nature's own humor, just take a wild ride!

Nature's Youngest Bard

A tiny sprout with dreams so bold,
  Whispers tales of legends old.
With leaves as pages, life is bright,
  In the sun, it dances with delight.

Its laughter echoes, ticks and tocks,
  Tickling roots and teasing rocks.
A playful breeze, the bard's own voice,
  Singing tunes of nature's choice.

Pages of Petals

In the garden, wild tales bloom,
Where petals scribble, dispelling gloom.
A daisy wrote a joke today,
About a bee who forgot the way.

Buttercups chuckle, giggles ensue,
As daisies hitch a ride in dew.
Their pages flutter in the breeze,
Sharing secrets with buzzing bees.

Musings of the Meadow

In the meadow, where mischief thrives,
Grass blades gossip; oh, how they jive!
A clover claims it's lucky, you see,
While a dandelion fluffs in glee.

With chatter loud, they spread the word,
A worm just found a giant bird!
And as the sun dips low and red,
The flowers chuckle in their bed.

Budding Inspirations

Tiny buds with whispers sweet,
Dreaming hard on summer's heat.
A crocus thinks it's quite the star,
While ants march by, a busy bazaar.

Leaves scribble thoughts on breezy days,
Composing tunes in leafy ways.
Bright blooms nod, they join the fun,
In this garden dance under the sun.

Brushstrokes of Blooming Hope

A little seed has big dreams,
It hopes to paint the world in greens.
With crayons made of sunshine bright,
It splashes joy—what a silly sight!

The roots dance down to make a scene,
While leaves wiggle in a playful glean.
They joke about the clouds up high,
And whisper secrets to the sky.

Each petal wears a goofy grin,
Spreading cheer from within.
The world's a canvas to be filled,
With laughter from the garden, thrilled!

Treetop Thoughts

In the treetop, birds like to chat,
About a squirrel dressed in a hat.
They joke of acorns, big and round,
And wonder where the lost ones found.

Branches creak with giggling glee,
As they share tales of roly-poly.
The breeze tickles leaves up high,
Causing branches to sway and sigh.

They ponder if the sun is shy,
Or just too busy in the sky.
In the company of feathered friends,
A day of fun will never end!

Unfolding Stories of Spring

A butterfly writes poetry in flight,
Each stanza swirling, oh what a sight!
With colorful ink and a twirl,
It dances around, giving flowers a whirl.

A ladybug pens a memoir bold,
Of love and adventures untold.
With spots of mirth, it turns the page,
While the daisies laugh and join the stage!

They giggle at raindrops that slip,
Creating puddles for a playful dip.
Each bloom adds lines to the rhyme,
In nature's book, it's springtime!

Ink and Photosynthesis

With pens made of petals, they sketch the day,
While sunlight giggles, dancing away.
The trees hold brushes, green and wide,
Creating canvases where critters hide.

A beetle with glasses writes witty prose,
About how the garden always grows.
It catches ink from the dew each morn,
Joking that it was a flower reborn!

Each stem is a writer, each leaf a sage,
Turning nature into a vibrant page.
With roots and shoots, their stories blend,
In a world of twirls, where whimsy won't end.

Fresh Beginnings

In the garden of my dreams,
Little sprouts plot funny schemes.
They wiggle, they giggle, so spry,
With roots that reach for the sky.

A daisy wears a sun hat wide,
While a weed tries to take a ride.
The cabbages crack jokes so loud,
Making the tulips laugh so proud.

Fragile Ends

When leaves start to turn to dust,
Fungi dance without a fuss.
A spider weaves a tale or two,
With silken threads and morning dew.

The crickets sing their last refrain,
While pumpkins laugh at falling rain.
Things wither and sigh, how absurd,
Each whisper shared, not a word heard.

The Hum of New Life

A caterpillar wears a crown,
While ants march joyfully down.
The bees buzz gossip in the air,
Sharing secrets without a care.

Seedlings break through, a silly sight,
With tiny hats, oh what a fright!
A worm winks and does a jig,
While the birds cheer, 'What a big gig!'

Verses Between the Vines

Between the rows of green and gold,
The stories of the weeds unfold.
They jest and jive with each small sprout,
As Mother Nature laughs, no doubt.

The grape leaves giggle, grow quite high,
While squirrels plan their next supply.
A tangle here, a twist there, too,
All in the garden's playful view.

Shadows of Succulent Dreams

In the shade where cacti lounge,
Dreams sprout forth with a funny bounce.
The succulents host a dance tonight,
With party hats and laughter bright.

Lizards peep from behind the spines,
Cracking jokes in rhythmic lines.
A sweet aroma fills the air,
As blooming laughter starts to flare.

New Heights of Green

In the garden where I play,
Little leaves have much to say.
A curious bug with a tiny hat,
Claims he's the king of where it's at.

Sunflowers grin, they stand so tall,
While pepper plants play catch and ball.
A willow whispers, 'Let's have a dance!'
And all the sprouts just giggle and prance.

The daisies wear shoes made of dew,
While carrots dream of skies so blue.
Potatoes laugh in their hidden beds,
As veggies joke 'bout their fancy spreads.

With every twist and every twirl,
The garden's a jolly, greenish whirl.
A riot of nature, what a sight!
The best of days from morning to night.

Imprints of Innocence

Tiny hands leave prints in mud,
Creating chaos with the smallest thud.
A butterfly flutters by so fast,
'Try to catch me!' it dares, then laughs.

The ants hold meetings in crooked lines,
Debating on who gets the best vines.
A ladybug boasts of flying speed,
While crickets chirp, 'Let us take heed!'

Dandelions sprout, their wishes untold,
As children giggle, brave and bold.
Every stumble and tumble, a happy sound,
In this patch of dreams where joy is found.

Sprouts send giggles up to the sky,
While flowers wink and butterflies fly.
A silly dance 'neath clouds that sway,
Childhood whispers, 'Let's play all day!'

Words Among the Weeds

In tangled grass where secrets grow,
The weeds conspire with the wind's soft blow.
A minuscule frog croaks out a joke,
While bees gossip, spreading word smoke.

'What's green and has four wheels?' they tease,
'A rolly-polly bus, if you please!'
The flowers chuckle, the roots stay sly,
With humor blooming as they pass by.

The tulips droop in silent mirth,
As laughter echoes across the earth.
'Why did the plant hide in the dirt?
To avoid the paparazzi's flirt!'

Beneath the leaves, a story unfolds,
Of jokes and giggles that nature holds.
Each handy tale a fit for glee,
In the riotous world of green esprit.

Corners of the Canopy

In shady spots where giggles bloom,
The branches sway, dispelling gloom.
A squirrel jests with acorns galore,
'Who needs nuts? Let's dance on the floor!'

With sunbeams filtering through the leaves,
The forest whispers as mischief weaves.
A raccoon dives into a pile of trash,
Claiming he's found a treasure stash!

Birds are chirping a silly tune,
While shadows play beneath the moon.
'Why do trees never get lost at sea?
Because they always branch out to be free!'

In corners where laughter meets the trees,
The canopy shakes with a playful breeze.
Nature's choir fills the air,
With jokes and giggles everywhere.

Tangled Tales of Growth

In a pot, a sprout did dance,
It tripped on roots, took a chance.
With leaves that wobbled all around,
It lost a shoe without a sound.

The garden gnomes began to cheer,
As veggies giggled, loud and clear.
A worm in boots, a sight to see,
Declaring, "Dance, oh sprout, with glee!"

The sun forgot his usual glow,
And tickled leaves from down below.
Grasshoppers joined in on the fun,
While ladybugs led everyone.

Then came the rain, a slippery mess,
Each tiny plant in wet distress.
But with a splash, they made a play,
Turning muddy fears to a frolic day.

Doodles in the Dirt

In the dirt, a doodle sprouted,
With scribbles on the ground, it shouted:
"I'm not just any plant, you see,
I'm the doodle king, just plant me!"

The carrot said, "Don't get ahead,
You're just a line, not even red!"
The tomato blushed, a rosy hue,
"Doodle or not, we'll grow with you!"

A radish rolled its tiny eyes,
"Let's scribble plans that touch the skies."
With leafy friends who gigged and squiggled,
Their garden plot was truly wiggles.

Through rainy days, and sunny glares,
They giggled loud, forgot their cares.
For in the dirt, each jest unfurled,
The funniest garden in the world!

Verses from the Garden's Heart

Amidst the blooms, a chatter rose,
As daisies laughed at all the prose.
"Who knew we'd be the poets here?"
A sunflower laughed, "Let's share some cheer!"

The carrots rapped a funky beat,
While peas jumped high, with nimble feet.
"Plant life's too short for solemn thoughts,"
Chimed in the beans, with clever knots.

A pumpkin claimed a glorious crown,
"I'm the jester of this leafy town!"
But melons smiled, so round and bright,
"We'll roll with laughter, day and night!"

From roots to shoots, joy took its aim,
Each verse a giggle, each plant a name.
In this garden of humor, dreams ignite,
Where laughter blooms, and everything feels right!

Chronicles of the Seedling

A seedling snuck out late at night,
Dreaming of stars that shone so bright.
It tried to dance, but fell with a thud,
And rolled right into a muddy puddle of mud.

The friendly weeds all gathered round,
Creating a band, a silly sound.
With twigs for guitars, they twanged away,
While bugs formed a crowd for their cabaret!

"What's this jam?" asked a nosy snail,
"The coolest gig, you'll hear the tale!"
And off went fireflies, lighting the show,
With every flicker, the giggles did grow.

But as the dawn began to glow,
The seedling yawned, "Oh dear, oh no!"
With squeezing roots, it found its place,
In this garden, laughter's no race!

Whispers of Young Leaves

In the garden, giggles grow,
Tiny shoots put on a show.
Leafy whispers, secrets shared,
Beneath the sun, they dance unpaired.

Wiggling worms wear hats of soil,
As raindrops join in on the toil.
They plot adventures, oh so grand,
On tiny branches, life is planned.

Gusts of wind bring out the glee,
Swirling foliage, wild and free.
They tickle bees and tease the sun,
In this green realm, all is fun.

Though storms may try to shake them down,
Young leaves wear nature's finest crown.
With every gust, they laugh and sway,
In the breeze, they find their way.

Fledgling Ink on Earth

A little sprout with dreams of flight,
Doodles in the dirt, what a sight!
With mud as paper, worms as pens,
Writing stories with all their friends.

Rabbits hop by, oh what a tease,
Knocking over ink with such ease.
Little roots shout, 'Hey, that's not fair!'
As petals giggle high in the air.

In the sun's rays, they craft a tale,
Of fluffy clouds and a fluffy snail.
The soil's laughter, rich and deep,
Echoes around as they all leap.

As evening falls with an orange hue,
The drawings fade, but dreams renew.
Tomorrow brings more art to show,
In the patch of dirt where laughter flow.

The Blossom's First Words

A bud once shy begins to speak,
'Watch me bloom, this won't be bleak!'
With petals bright, it tells the tale,
Of sunny skies and breezy gales.

Little bees buzz, 'What's your name?'
The blossom giggles, 'I'm not the same!'
Each color whispers, tales in bloom,
Fun in the garden, no time for gloom.

Nectar spills, a sugary treat,
Attracting critters, all take their seat.
They gather round for the big reveal,
In this floral drama, joy is real.

With every petal, a story grows,
Of adventurers where the river flows.
And as the sun begins to fade,
The blossom laughs at this grand parade.

Roots Beneath the Page

Below the soil, a party's held,
Roots sing songs, all tales are yelled.
They scribble secrets, plant their dreams,
In earthy rhythms, laughter streams.

They spill their ink in playful swirls,
Telling tales of whirling twirls.
With twigs like quills, they craft their lore,
Of snails on journeys, oh what a score!

Shadows dance and sunlight beams,
While critters share their wildest schemes.
Among the dirt, the roots entwine,
Writing stories, oh so divine.

In this hidden realm of delight,
Where whispers echo into the night.
Every word, a treasure trove,
As life unfolds, in roots, we rove.

Petal-Powered Poetry

In a garden where giggles bloom,
Petals dance like a silly broom.
Bees wear hats, a buzzing spree,
While flowers laugh in harmony.

Butterflies join the crazy ride,
Swirling colors far and wide.
A daffodil in polka dots,
Says, "Life's better with funny thoughts!"

Worms recite their wriggly verse,
In the dirt, they're quite perverse.
Grinning gnomes on mushroom chairs,
Giggle at the bunnies' dares.

When rain drops join the jolly song,
Splashes dance where they belong.
With each splash, the garden sways,
Living out its quirky ways.

The Child's Orchard

In the orchard where laughter grows,
Giggling apples strike silly poses.
A child swings from a bough so high,
Tickling clouds in the bright blue sky.

Cherries wear their party hats,
While pears pull pranks on curious cats.
The branches shake with playful glee,
As juicy secrets spill from each tree.

A squirrel juggles acorns in glee,
While singing tunes, oh so carefree.
Lemonade rivers flow nearby,
Inviting all to snack and fly.

In this grove of silly delight,
Monkeys swing from day to night.
The child smiles with mischief galore,
In the orchard, who could ask for more?

The Poetry of Tiny Shoots

Tiny shoots with so much sass,
Wobble in the morning grass.
They play hopscotch with the dew,
Watching clouds drift, giggle too.

A beetle wears a jaunty tie,
While grasshoppers leap up high.
Finding joy in every inch,
Each sprout and sprig has a funny pinch.

Ladybugs whisper funny fables,
As dandelions spin like labels.
The wind joins in, a chuckle or two,
Tickling leaves as the sun breaks through.

Each little shoot has grand dreams,
Of seeing worlds beyond their beams.
With every sway, they twist and shout,
In the garden, there's never doubt!

Reflections of a Verdant Dream

In the dream where greens reside,
Trees wear shades with great pride.
Silly shadows tickle the ground,
Whispering jokes all around.

Flowers flaunt their vibrant flair,
While suns and moons play truth or dare.
A toad croaks like a stand-up star,
As the wind joins in from afar.

Breezes bring the latest news,
About the best tree-jumping views.
With each rustle, gossip flows,
As nature giggles, and laughter grows.

In this verdant world so grand,
Every leaf has its own band.
Each reflection holds a giddy tune,
Nature's theater under the moon.

Verses of Verdancy

In a garden so lush, where the weeds like to dance,
A flower once tripped, gave a deer quite a chance.
It giggled and fell, on a soft patch of moss,
'Watch where you step! I'm not here for your toss!'

The insects held court on a leaf oh so wide,
Debating if clouds made for better hide.
A ladybug blushed, said, 'I'm quite the belle!'
While the ants in the back thought they'd all cast a spell.

A sunflower stretched, with a grin full of cheer,
Said, 'Sun is my jam, and I'm drinking quite near!'
But a cloud rolled in quick, made the sun swipe a frown,
'This moisture is nice, but I hate wearing brown!'

When evening arrives, and the critters all rhyme,
They share silly tales with pure, jingling chime.
Laughter erupts, as the fireflies buzz,
'In this colorful world, who needs more than just us?'

The Grace of Greenery

A cabbage once pondered, 'Am I leafy or round?'
As the carrots around just spun round and around.
'We're not meant for twirling!' a beetroot exclaimed,
But the cabbage was lost, clearly still a bit shamed.

A tree nearby shouted, 'Oi! Keep it down, please!'
But his branches were swaying like a fresh autumn breeze.
With a rustle and giggle, the leaves told the tale,
Of the day that the wind thought it might play the snail.

In a patch of green gallows, the green beans took flight,
With a mission to find out who was spicy, who lightweight!
A pepper piped up, in a suit made of zest,
'I'm hot on the trail; come along for the quest!'

From the soil to the sky, each plant had its role,
Each one with a quirk, together a whole.
Through jokes and jests, they bound through the night,
In the garden of giggles, everything feels right.

Sprouting Songlines

A little sprout sang softly to the soil below,
'If you could sing back, just let your roots grow!'
But the earth just chuckled, a bass full of puns,
'Oh dear little sprout, I'm here just for fun!'

The flowers in bloom joined the sprout's merry tune,
Came what danced, the daisies, under the moon.
They giggled through petals, and swayed in delight,
With each little breeze, they took flight in the night.

To the frogs by the pond, they hollered 'Give heed!'
'You're staying too still, it's funny indeed!'
A frog cleared his throat, and began to croon,
'We'll perform at the ball, just give us a boon!'

A chorus of seeds began to take shape,
Through laughter and whimsy, in vibrant escape.
With roots intertwining and leaves full of might,
They swayed as one family, under the moonlight.

Tender Tinctures

In a patchwork of colors, the veggies began,
To chatter and giggle, through each little plan.
Carrots spread tales of their high-flying grace,
While radishes blushed, hiding their purple face.

An onion once swore he could dance like a pro,
But each time he moved, he would just start to glow!
'The more that I twirl, the more I shall weep!'
So the rest all just laughed as they tried not to creep.

A pickle declared, 'I'll be king of this patch!'
'Though my brine's quite a scent, it's a wonderful catch!'
But the tomatoes just giggled, rolled under their vines,
'You think you're the best? Well, we make great wines!'

And as twilight fell, each color took flight,
In the canvas of nature, nothing felt tight.
With laughter as paint, they created a thrill,
In the garden of giggles, they danced 'til the chill.

Lively Lines of Nature

In the garden, bugs wear hats,
Dancing 'round with chatter and spats.
The flowers giggle with surprise,
As the sun winks from the skies.

Squirrels read their acorn books,
While hiding in the sunny nooks.
The grass tickles the wandering feet,
Nature's humor is quite a treat!

Bees hold court, buzzing their tales,
While the breeze carries cheerful gales.
Each leaf rustles with a grin,
Sharing secrets held within.

The clouds puff out, feeling brave,
As the wind rides them like a wave.
With laughter, nature tells a tale,
Of lively lines on a bright green trail.

A Leaf's Gentle Musings

A leaf sighed as it caught the sun,
Oh, the blessings of having fun!
It twirled down on a little whim,
Chasing shadows along the brim.

With a paper boat, it sailed away,
On a pond where frogs love to play.
Every ripple held a rhyme,
And time seemed to slow down in prime.

Whispers floated through the trees,
Tickling branches in the breeze.
When it rained, oh what a show!
Each drop a giggle, singing low.

At dusk, it settled, tired but bright,
Dreaming of adventures in the night.
As the stars winked at its tale,
A leaf laughed loud, it could not fail.

Writing Under the Canopy

Beneath the branches, a writer sighs,
With a notebook full of silly lies.
A raccoon peeks, curious and spry,
As the ink flows like clouds in the sky.

The squirrels help with a dash of spice,
Adding acorn jokes, oh so nice!
Each page flickers with laughter and cheer,
As critters gather to lend an ear.

A butterfly flits, critiquing the plot,
While ants march lines, taking a shot.
The mushrooms giggle, inspire a scene,
Telling stories of where they've been.

With each word penned, the joy just grows,
In a world where only nature knows.
As twilight dances, the tales take flight,
Under the canopy, filled with delight.

The Words of Wild Beginnings

In the meadow, all creatures convene,
To share their tales, and it's quite the scene!
The grasshopper sings with a hop and a skip,
While a wise old owl offers a quip.

A rabbit brings snacks, a carrot delight,
While the daisies gossip in the soft twilight.
Each bloom offers wisdom, wrapped in chuckles,
As hedgehogs snicker, tangled in cuddles.

Even the rocks chip in with their views,
A stalactite joke that gets some moos.
The laughter ripples like a bubbling brook,
In the heart of nature, where fun is the hook.

With a final cheer, the sun bids adieu,
As bedtime stories float in the dew.
With every whisper of the wild winds' spin,
The world giggles, ready to begin.

Echoes of a Young Seedling

In the soil, a sprout did rise,
Tickling worms with leafy ties.
It whispered jokes to passing breeze,
Poking fun at buzzing bees.

With roots that danced a silly jig,
And leaves that waved like a friendly fig.
It giggled loud when raindrops fell,
Singing songs of the earth's sweet smell.

Chasing shadows as sunbeams flashed,
Making faces as clear skies clashed.
What secrets does the young one keep?
Dreams of trees and naps that leap.

Buddies with rocks, they sit and plot,
Growing wise in the very spot.
A tiny voice with tales to tell,
Of muddy mischiefs that went so well.

A Budding Tale

A little sprout with big dreams spry,
Told the clouds, "I'm gonna fly!"
With leaves for wings and roots like feet,
It twirled around in a leafy beat.

It peeked at bugs all scurrying fast,
Said, "Hurry up, at least don't last!"
While ants were marching in a line,
The sprout would giggle, feeling divine.

Its dreams were grand, as seeds can be,
Imagining heights above the tree.
With each new bud, it cracked a grin,
Saying, "With this, let the fun begin!"

A tale not told by wizened trees,
But by the laughter carried in breeze.
For in the garden, fun's the aim,
With every sprout, it's just the same.

Unfurling Leaves of Imagination

One fine morning, fresh and bright,
A young leaf dreamed of taking flight.
With a whoosh and a flurry, it jumped in glee,
Imagining the sky, a home for a leafy spree.

"Look at me, I'm a flying kite!"
Shouted the shoot, with all its might.
But the wind just laughed, as leaves tend to do,
"We're not that brave, we're not so new!"

A squirrel heard and raised an ear,
"Join with me, we'll have no fear!"
And the new leaves cheered, roaring with fun,
As rules of the garden began to bend and run.

Together they danced in the sun's warm light,
Making shadows that jumped with delight.
In the magic of green, their dreams took flight,
Unfurling laughter that felt just right.

Galactic Green

A sprout announced, "I'm from outer space!"
With a twinkling leaf and a sprightly grace.
It floated down on a comet's tail,
Chasing moonbeams with a giddy wail.

"Watch me shine, I could glow all night!"
Exclaimed the bud, feeling just right.
With stars for friends, it told grand tales,
Of cosmic winds and comet trails.

"Plant me here, I'll start a trend,
Of intergalactic friends 'til the end!"
The daisies rolled their eyes in jest,
"Here comes the sprout with its wild quest!"

But in the heart of the garden's green,
Laughter burst forth, bright and keen.
For every seedling, no matter where,
Hopes and giggles float in the air.

Nature's Childish Prose

In a garden, a gnome lost his hat,
He borrowed a leaf from a plump little cat.
The daisies giggled, the bees made a buzz,
While the tree trunk laughed, 'What a sight! Just because!'

A squirrel juggling acorns fell with a thud,
His pals yelled, 'Get up, you're covered in mud!'
The robins were chuckling, flapping their wings,
As the sun poked out, revealing such things.

The wind told a tale of dancing elks,
It whirled through the branches, playing with kelks.
But the brook rolled its eyes, said, 'What do you know?',
'Let me run fast; there's nowhere to go!'

So nature keeps scribbling, with joy in each sprawl,
With laughter and mischief, it beckons us all.

Language of the Living Woods

In the heart of the woods, a raccoon took flight,
On a kite made of leaves, oh what a sight!
The owls gave a hoot, the snakes did a dance,
While the trees shook their branches in merry romance.

A porcupine wiggled, as sharp as she got,
Claiming the crown of a spiky mascot.
The ferns all adorned in their feathered best,
Cried out, 'Join the fun! Take part in our fest!'

Squirrels were tweeting their favorite tunes,
The mushrooms were grooving—oh, under the moons!
They shared secret wishes as fireflies glowed,
Each flicker a word, a story bestowed.

The trees whispered secrets, the bushes could sing,
Let's frolic together, with joy that we bring!
In the language of nature, we all join the spree,
With laughter in leaves and purest joy, you see.

Whispers of New Growth

A tiny green shoot peeked out from the dirt,
It noticed the sun and squealed, 'I'm alert!'
The raindrops giggled, 'Welcome to the show!'
'Let's sprout some fun, let's stir up a glow!'

The worms made a parade, all slimy and bright,
Said, 'Join us, dear sprout, it'll be quite a sight!'
The daisies all danced, their petals a-spread,
While the beetles agreed, 'Let's party instead!'

With whispers of breezes that tickled each leaf,
They tickled the roots, spreading glee and belief.
The young buds all laughed, oh what a delight,
As they swayed to the rhythm of day turning night.

Each blush of the bloom made the garden alive,
A symphony vibrant where all creatures thrive.
With whispers of laughter, the sprouts found their way,
In the gentle embrace of a bright, sunny day.

Tender Roots and Dreams

Down in the earth where the giggles reside,
The roots tell their tales where the worms like to hide.
The pebbles react to each tiny detail,
As the snails write their stories, oh, slow like a snail!

The sunbeams bring laughter, a tickle or two,
To every young bud that pops out to view.
The daisies parade in their polka-dot best,
Waving at ladybugs, oh what a fest!

Up high in the branches, a party unfolds,
With the chattering sparrows and shy little folds.
They share all their dreams of the skies and the trees,
With whispers of magic that float in the breeze.

So come join the fun in this whimsical land,
Where dreams intertwine with the joys that we've planned.
In the roots and the leaves, let the laughter resound,
For nature's a playground where joy can be found.

In the Shade of Tiny Leaves

A critter in a sun hat, oh what a sight,
Sipping lemonade, feeling just right.
His shadow's a dance, a jig on the grass,
While ants march by, oh how they all pass.

With whispers of wind, they chat about snacks,
Pinecones and acorns, shushing the wacks.
A squirrel chimes in, with a nutty old tale,
Of stealing a sandwich, his own little grail.

Then comes the sun, bright as can be,
"Who turned the lights on?" shouts Bumblebee.
Their laughter erupts, a chorus of glee,
In the shade of their haven, so wild and so free.

Seasonal Musings

In spring, the flowers just can't hold their cheer,
A daisy bounces, "Hey, summer is near!"
The tulips giggle, their colors a glow,
While bees engage in a buzzing ballet show.

As summer rolls in, the sun's in a haze,
A tomato blushes, brings heat to its phase.
Corn's got a dance, it sways with the breeze,
Chasing the raindrops; life's just a tease!

When autumn arrives, it's a wobbly flight,
Leaves twirl and tumble, a dazzling sight.
Pumpkins sing songs, with spice in the air,
While critters in jackets prepare for the fair.

Then winter sets in, all snuggled and nice,
Snowmen do pirouettes, they dance on the ice.
A bear's hibernating; where is his snack?
Dreaming of spring when the sun will come back!

The Language of Blossoms

Roses whisper secrets, tulips give a wink,
In petals they giggle, oh, what do they think?
Dandelions chuckle, their wishes in flight,
While lilies put on the best floral fright!

A daffodil shouts, "Let's brighten the day!"
With a nod from the violets, they join in the play.
Petunia jokes softly, her laughter's a breeze,
While daisies debate about who's got the keys!

Chrysanthemums clash with a pollen puffed fight,
But hug it all out under soft moonlight.
In the garden, they prance, in colors so grand,
Each bloom is a joker with a whimsical hand!

Whimsical Woods

In the woods where the giggles are hidden from sight,
The trees tell tales with their branches at night.
A fox with a cap, oh, isn't he sly?
He's planning a party, I wonder, oh my!

Squirrels swing high, they're acrobat kings,
While owls play chess, tossing wisdom like flings.
Raccoons in bandanas are dancing like stars,
They're crafting a symphony with sticks and with jars.

The mushrooms are laughing, they're tickled with dew,
While toadstools compare hats; can yours beat my hue?
A rabbit who juggles keeps throwing out greens,
In whimsical woods where laughter convenes!

Footprints in the Soil

In muddy paths we prance and play,
With squishy shoes that make us sway.
We laugh at footprints left behind,
A silly dance, oh, how we're twined!

A worm chases us, we run, we dash,
Through grass and dirt, we make a splash.
Our giggles echo, wild and free,
Nature's stage is where we'll be!

The bugs are starring in our show,
With tiny costumes, stealing the glow.
As we create our muddy art,
The laughter flows, it warms the heart!

So next time you step out to roam,
Just remember, the earth's your home.
Leave your mark, let your joy unfurl,
In every step, in every whirl!

Growing Up in Verse

In a garden where dreams take root,
We scribble lines in shiny loot.
A daisy chews on a thoughtful pen,
It writes a tale of flowered zen!

With puns and giggles, the petals sway,
In verses bright, they dance and play.
The bees all buzz a jolly song,
As nature joins our verse so strong!

Each sprout has secrets to share and keep,
Under the stars, when the world's asleep.
We trade our tales, a leafy riff,
In laughter's glow, we write our gift!

So gather 'round to hear the cheer,
Our garden tales, they bring you near.
With every rhyme, we grow and jest,
In the land of green, we are truly blessed!

Seeds Beneath the Surface

Beneath the dirt, where whispers dwell,
Seeds tell stories, oh-so swell.
They giggle softly, "What will we be?"
"A flower, a tree, or perhaps a pea?"

In the silence, thoughts start to sprout,
"Should we be radishes, or twist and shout?"
With tiny roots that stretch and squirm,
They ponder their fate, their earthy firm!

The rain arrives, a slimy friend,
Shouting, "Grow up, it's time to blend!"
In puddles deep, they start to play,
These little seeds have much to say!

They burst with laughter as they unfurl,
Turning into something quite a whirl.
From the depths, they rise with glee,
Oh, the wonders we're destined to see!

A Journey Through Foliage

Through leaves and branches, we shall wander,
In a leafy maze, our hearts grow fonder.
With arms wide open, we take a chance,
A step, a skip, a clumsy dance!

The squirrels chatter, "What's your plan?"
As we twirl beneath the grand oak span.
"We're just here, to giggle and glide,
In nature's lap, where joy can't hide!"

With every rustle, we hear the calls,
Of critters and birds that craft their brawls.
A flower giggles, "Join the spree!"
As we tiptoe past, so wild and free!

In this lush land, we feel so bold,
With funny tales in roots we mold.
So grab a leaf and join the fun,
Our journey's bright, it's just begun!

Petals in the Wind

A flower sneezed and blew away,
Leaving bees to dance and play.
The tulips giggled in soft flair,
While daisies tossed out petals in the air.

A squirrel laughed, a chipmunk grinned,
Together they sketched the breeze to send.
With every swirl and twirl they made,
Nature's laughter in the sun displayed.

The roses twirled, what a wild sight,
Dancing off in morning light.
Each colored petal told a tale,
As butterflies rode on a laughing gale.

Oh, what a show these blossoms bring,
When the wind, like a joker, starts to sing.
They leap and spin like silly folk,
In a garden dressed for the finest joke.

Inked Dreams of Greenery

With quill in hand and ink in bloom,
A toad declared, "Let's paint the room!"
He dipped his feet in shades so bright,
And swirled about, a comical sight.

The leaves all chuckled, "What a mess!"
As frogs made splatters in their dress.
A painter's palette turned to glee,
In every stroke, pure comedy.

A hedgehog joined with spiked delight,
To draw a sun that shone so bright.
He rolled and jiggled, left his mark,
Creating giggles 'til it got dark.

The canvas grew with laughter's flow,
As nature danced, its colors aglow.
Each mark a smile, each hue a grin,
In a world where joy and whim begin.

Sketches of Sprouting Life

Tiny sprouts with eyes so wide,
Sketching dreams where worms reside.
Each leaf a page from nature's book,
With giggles hiding in every nook.

A beetle posed, a model proud,
As ants scuttled 'neath the crowd.
Playful doodles in the dirt,
Making art with nature's flirt.

Cotton clouds above them smiled,
A painter's brush, nature's wild child.
With laughter sprouting on the ground,
An artist's bloom of joy was found.

Oh, what fun these sprigs can play,
Creating mischief day by day.
With each new bud, a funny tale,
Of life's bright antics on the trail.

Nature's New Narratives

In the forest's heart, tales unfold,
As critters gather, life's stories told.
A rabbit hops and starts to prance,
While squirrels chatter, lost in dance.

Each branch a stage for frogs to croak,
Their rhythmic beats a jolly joke.
The flowers sway with tales of cheer,
Turning blossoms into laughter's sphere.

A wise old owl winks and sways,
As he recounts his starry days.
With tales of mischief, fun and games,
Each colorful critter, known by names.

So let them share their woodsy lore,
In this grand play we all adore.
For every leaf and petal grand,
Is a laugh served up by nature's hand.

Echoes of Tender Growth

In the garden where giggles sprout,
A lettuce whispers, "What's that about?"
Tiny roots dance in a silly parade,
Worms giggle, while plotting their jade escapade.

The daisies discuss their fashion flair,
"Those ants, do they really think they're a pair?"
Each leaf gives a nod, trying hard not to grin,
While the sunflower complains, "I need some sunscreen!"

Little sprouts trade secrets at dusk,
Offering up jokes with a ripe, leafy husk.
With whispers of pollen and breezy delight,
They plan a crop party that pops in the night.

As the moon watches over this cheerful zone,
The radish sings soft—a humorous tone.
In the patch where laughter grows wild and free,
Life's just a joke on a bright, leafy spree.

Letters from the Understory

Dear Beetle, I've scribbled in ink of the night,
The mushrooms were laughing, oh, what a sight!
Your shoes are outdated, I must make it clear,
But your dance moves? My friend, those we cheer!

The rabbits were giggling at shadows they chase,
While squirrels exchanged fashion tips at their pace.
I wrote down my dreams while sipping on dew,
Next week, I'll wear petals. What will you do?

Ferns gave me wisdom wrapped snug in a leaf,
They chuckled at worries, so small and so brief.
The hedgehog chimed in, with a snicker and jest,
"Beneath all your spines, it's fun to be a guest!"

In the whispers of vines that tangle and twine,
All nature confirms, that humor's divine!
So here's to the trees that sway with delight,
Their letters of laughter, sung bold in the night.

The Joy of Budding Verses

I once saw a cactus with great tales to tell,
About all its friends, living under its shell.
Cherries on branches, laughing with glee,
They joke 'bout the bees, "They're just too busy!"

A sunflower stood tall with a grin on its face,
"It's tough being bright, but I've found my place!"
While daisies were bouncing, comparing their heights,
"Let's race to the top!" was their silly invite.

The breeze brought a giggle, a chuckle from leaves,
As critters debated whose home to believe.
Roots tangled and twisted, an odd kind of art,
Each whispered a secret, here no one's apart.

So here's to the laughter that blossoms and grows,
With puns and with pranks, nature's comic prose.
In every small petal, in each twinkling sprout,
The joy of these verses is what it's about!

Sprouts of Imagination

In a patch of lost dreams, sprouts giggle and play,
They dream of the clouds, drifting softly away.
"Wouldn't it be great," said a daring young sprout,
"To swap all these roots for a wild, jumpy route?"

The carrots are plotting their grand escape plan,
While the chives just can't help but develop a fan.
They pen down their visions on leaves oh so bright,
And dream of a dance party under moonlight!

Each seedling envisions its future so grand,
To tickle the sky or explore distant sand.
With laughter infectious, inspired dreams twirl,
Nature's young jokers, in a magical whirl.

And when the sun sets, painting skies in gold,
The roots giggle secrets, the stories unfold.
Imagination sprouts in each nook and each bend,
In the garden of dreams, the fun never ends!

Growing Pains of the Forest

In the forest lush and gay,
The trees complain about their sway.
"I'm taller than you, just you wait!"
They laugh and tease about their fate.

Bark is peeling, limbs a-flail,
"I'm losing leaves, I'm going pale!"
A squirrel chuckles from his nest,
"Nature's here to put you to the test!"

Rooted firmly, trees did bicker,
Some grew slow, while others quicker.
"You've lost your fluff!" the willow cried,
"At least I'm here, with nothing to hide!"

Finally, they learned with time,
Each has a style, a grand design.
Humorous roots, they stretched and played,
In this silly wood, they laughed all day!

The Poetry of Petals

Petals pirouette in glee,
Dancing breezes tickle free.
"I'm the pinkest of them all!"
"Not with that dirt, you might just fall!"

Sunflowers turn with silly zeal,
"I'm the tallest!" they appeal.
Roses giggle, thorns on show,
"Only pretty ones can glow!"

Honeybees buzz in delight,
"Oh, flower friends, what a sight!"
"Who's the sweetest?" they all plead,
"Let's just pollinate, yes indeed!"

In this patch of blooms so bright,
Nature's jest, a whimsical sight.
With laughter shared, the colors blend,
In floral fun, the joy won't end!

Tender Tendrils

Little vines around trees twist,
"I'm so strong!" they can't resist.
"Oh really? Just look at me!"
"I'm growing up, can't you see?"

Hugging branches, oh so tight,
Trying hard to reach the light.
"You're creeping up! You look so small!"
"I'm just warming up, that's all!"

They stretch out in a green parade,
Making shapes in sun and shade.
"Do you think we'll touch the sky?"
"Only if we try, oh my!"

Giggles echo through the leaves,
Nature's whimsy never grieves.
With every twist, they claim their place,
In this viney, fun embrace!

Twisting Vines of Thought

In the garden of the mind,
Thoughts through twisting vines unwind.
"I'm a genius!" one proclaimed,
"But what if I'm just too untamed?"

Each idea sprouts something new,
"I'll climb higher than you do!"
Riddles wrap around so sly,
"Let's unravel, oh my, oh my!"

Tangled dreams flit through the air,
"Do you think that's just unfair?"
"Let's knot them up, make a mess!
It's more fun, I must confess!"

A riot of colors, thoughts collide,
With laughter echoing, they abide.
In this garden, joy they sought,
Twisting vines are what they brought!

From Bud to Blossom

A little bud with dreams so wild,
It giggles softly, just a child.
With sunshine's kiss and rain's embrace,
It bursts with laughter, taking its place.

Oh look, it bends to chat with bees,
Telling tales while swaying with ease.
A dancing green with wiggles and hops,
In the garden of joy, it never stops.

It tries on petals, bright and bold,
Wearing colors, oh so gold.
Each day a costume, full of flair,
Who knew a bud could be so rare?

So from bud to bloom, a journey starts,
With playful giggles, and happy hearts.
In the world of green, it's never grim,
Life's a garden, and we all should swim.

Sprout's Soliloquy

Once a seed in the dirt so deep,
Dreaming of the sky, taking a leap.
With a wiggle and a squirm, it starts to sprout,
Whispering secrets, there's no doubt.

"Look at me! I'm stretching wide!"
Doing the cha-cha on nature's ride.
With quirky roots and funny leaves,
I'm the star on which nature weaves.

Tickled by the wind's soft song,
A sprout sings proudly, "I belong!"
Every drop of rain a splashy tune,
Dancing under the playful moon.

With sunlight giggles, I jump and play,
Sprouting dreams in a funny way.
Life's a laugh when you grow with glee,
A tiny sprout, so wild and free.

Syllables in the Soil

In the earth, where whispers dwell,
Each little seed has tales to tell.
With a plop and a plunk, they dive down deep,
Singing sweet songs, where silence sleeps.

"Hello, dear worms! Have you heard the news?"
They joke and giggle in their comfy shoes.
With dirt for blankets, they snuggle tight,
Creating poems all through the night.

Count the syllables in the row,
A rhythm in the soil, don't you know?
With roots for rhythm, and leaves for rhyme,
In the garden's heart, we dance in time.

So let's celebrate this funny crew,
With a chuckle here and a giggle too.
In every sprout, a story grows,
A symphony of laughter, everyone knows.

Memories of a Seed

Once a tiny speck on a breeze's whim,
Now a memory, oh so prim.
It chuckles softly, reminiscing days,
Of sunny dances in warm sun rays.

"I remember when I took a dive,
A leap of faith to feel alive!"
With dreams as vast as the endless sky,
It giggles at clouds drifting by.

Each little sprout a flashback spark,
Of cheeky roots playing in the dark.
From seed to plant, with laughter expressed,
It winks at nature, feeling blessed.

So here's to seeds, with stories to share,
In the garden of life, with laughter to spare.
Memories growing, fun never ends,
Celebrating life, with colorful friends.

Narratives of Nurture

In a pot sat a seed, quite proud,
Dreaming of rain and sunflower crowd.
It sprouted a leaf, looking so rad,
Said, "Look at me, I'm no longer a fad!"

A ladybug landed, with style and flair,
Offered its help to groom the hair.
"You're getting too big for this little pot,
Let's prank the garden, it'll be hot!"

The ants all gathered, with plans in mind,
"Let's throw a party, leave worries behind."
They danced 'round the roots, what a scene,
A festival of dirt, messy and green!

As night fell down, stars took their place,
The plants shared secrets, in their own space.
And through all the laughter, they felt quite spry,
A garden of giggles, reaching the sky.

The First Green

Once a tiny sprout with dreams so grand,
Thought it could dance across the land.
With each drop of dew and sunbeam's kiss,
It wriggled in joy, not wanting to miss.

A worm crawled by, with tales to tell,
Of jumping through puddles, feeling quite swell.
"Let's play hide and seek, just you and me,"
The sprout squealed, "Fine, but I'm hard to see!"

They played all day, till the moon rolled high,
The sprout claimed victory with a cheeky sigh.
"Next time," it laughed, "I'll grow taller still,
And you can't hide from my leafy thrill!"

With dreams of the sky and roots so bold,
The sprout kept playing, never growing old.
Each giggle echoed, through sunlight and rain,
In the garden of laughter, they'd entertain.

Garden of Words

In a patch of earth, words began to sprout,
Whispering secrets that made the world shout.
"Let's plant some jokes, right here in this row,
And see if their laughter will help us all grow!"

A pun was sown, and oh what a laugh,
The petals all shook at its clever craft.
"It tickles my roots, oh joyous delight,
Who knew garden talk could be such a fright?"

A rogue dandelion chimed in with flair,
"Let's spread this humor, it should go everywhere!"
With each gust of wind, laughter took flight,
And soon all the flowers bloomed with delight.

In this garden, where words took form,
Giggles and chuckles became the norm.
As butterflies danced, they knew what to do,
Breathe in that humor, let it sprout too!

Leaves of Laughter

A leaf on a branch, dressed up in green,
Declared, "In this garden, I'm the queen!"
It swayed with the breeze, danced to its tune,
Said, "Watch me shine, I'm the sun's monsoon!"

A squirrel scampered up, full of surprise,
"Your royal highness, with shimmering eyes.
Let's throw a bash with nuts and some treats,
Surely your reign brings the finest feats!"

The flowers all giggled, swaying in sync,
While bees joined in with their sweet honey drink.
"Let's make this a fest, with laughter and cheer,
For in this lush world, we've nothing to fear!"

As twilight settled, joy lit up the sky,
The garden erupted with each silly cry.
And through all the jests, beneath soft moon's light,
The leaves whispered fun, all through the night.

The Story of Tiny Twigs

Tiny twigs in a squiggly dance,
Wiggling around, they take a chance.
Swaying to tunes that no one can hear,
Tickled by breezes, they giggle with cheer.

One little twig thought it could fly,
Took off in a swoosh, but oh my, oh my!
Tumbled and rolled, made quite the fuss,
Landed with style in the roots of a bus!

Friends all around said, "What a brave move!"
While the leaves swayed with a playful groove.
Branching out boldly, they gave him a cheer,
The funniest twig with no trace of fear!

So remember this tale of the tiniest crew,
Dancing through life, oh what fun they do!
With laughter and joy, their antics don't lack,
Forever a twirling, giggling pack!

The Leaf's Lament

Oh woe is me, a leaf on a tree,
I yearn for a breeze, to set my soul free.
But every gust sends me flopping around,
A dance floor of chaos on the ground!

Once I was green, so vibrant, so bright,
Now I'm all crumpled, just not quite right.
My buddies all whisper, "Stick to your roots!"
While I play the part of old, rusty boots!

Falling's a trip, a comical sight,
Twirling and spinning, it's pure delight!
Shouting to squirrels, "Hey, watch where you land!
I may be all crinkly, but I'm still quite grand!"

So here I will laugh at my careless fall,
A tale of a leaf, once standing so tall.
With humor I bask in this autumn's embrace,
For life is a journey and I'm rolling with grace!

Sprouting Thoughts

In the garden of dreams, ideas will sprout,
Tiny seeds of laughter, that's what it's about.
Each thought like a bud, ready to bloom,
Tickling the air with a hint of perfume.

Plants whisper jokes that make flowers shake,
Giggling out loud at the moves that they make.
One sprout said, "Hey, let's prank the old tree,
Dress up as mushrooms and wait just to see!"

With chuckles and giggles, the leaves all turned red,
As the tree looked around, feeling quite misled.
But the joke was on them, he'd sprouted a grin,
"A well-played prank, I'll let the fun begin!"

So here in the garden of playful delight,
Funny little thoughts take off in flight.
With roots deep in laughter, they spread all around,
Sprouting up joy in the soft, leafy ground!

Dreams in the Sunshine

In the warmth of the sun, ideas ignite,
Little dreams chirping with pure delight.
Dancing on petals, in whimsical ways,
Spinning like tops in the sun's golden rays.

One flower declared, "Let's all tell a joke!
Why did the grasshopper jump over the oak?"
With giggles and snorts, the garden went wild,
As creatures conspired like a mischievous child!

"Let's hop in the breeze, we'll float like a kite!"
They fluttered and fluttered, oh what a sight!
But lo and behold, with the wind at their tails,
They tumbled and fumbled, like ships in gales!

So under the sun, in the soft afternoon,
The laughter grew louder, a joyous tune.
With dreams spinning circles, they leaped in delight,
In this sunny garden, everything's right!

Stems and Stories

In the garden where tales grow,
A tiny stalk wearing a bow.
It tells of a worm, kind of rude,
Who danced on my peas—what a mood!

A leaf with a laugh, oh so bright,
Claimed it could reach the sun tonight.
But instead, it tripped over a bee,
Who buzzed back, 'You're too young to be free!'

Saplings in a Summer Breeze

Two little buds play in the sun,
One says, 'Let's have some fun!'
They swayed and twirled with a skip,
Until a squirrel stole their drip!

The breeze tickled their leaves, they giggled,
As branches above subtly wiggled.
'Look, we're dancing!' one said with glee,
While the grass below sighed, 'Not for me!'

The Birth of Green Dreams

In a patch of earth, dreams took flight,
A seedling whispered, 'I'll grow overnight!'
But instead, it snoozed in the cool dirt,
Awakening later with a leaf that hurt.

It stretched high, then bumped a cloud,
'Hey, buddy, I'm trying to be loud!'
The cloud just grinned, a fluffy tease,
'You'll need a stronger root to please!'

Nature's First Breath

When the first sprout emerged from the gloom,
It sneezed and sent a flower to bloom.
'Excuse me,' it chuckled, trying to say,
'Guess I'm allergic to sunlight today!'

The breeze played along with a laugh,
As the weeds jokingly plotted their path.
'Let's race to the bug who took flight,'
'But watch your roots; they're a bit too light!'

www.ingramcontent.com/pod-product-compliance
Lightning Source LLC
Chambersburg PA
CBHW071844160426
43209CB00003B/407